Finding My Catholic Faith

Questions I Ask Myself

Finding My Catholic Faith

Questions I Ask Myself

For the Men and Women
in the Military Service
of the United States of America

Jude R. Senieur, Capuchin

Our Sunday Visitor
Publishing Division Huntington, Indiana

Nihil Obstat:
Rev. Michael J. Wrenn

Imprimi potest:
Rev. Robert L. McCreary, O.F.M. Cap.
Provincial, St. Augustine Province

Imprimatur:
♰ Joseph T. Ryan, D.D.
Archbishop of the Military Archdiocese
of the United States of America

Library of Congress Catalog Card Number:
85-62861
International Standard Book Number:
0-87973-224-5

Book design by Rebecca J. O'Brien

Published, printed and bound in the U.S.A. by
Our Sunday Visitor, Publishing Division
200 Noll Plaza
Huntington, Indiana 46750

224

*"How can they believe
unless they have heard?"*
                    Romans 10.14

To

JAN KLEINHESSELINK

Director of Religious Education
Twenty-five years of service
to military personnel and
their dependents.

Appreciation

Much time and effort has been put into the production of this little book by the following members of the military and their families to insure that the answers are readably clear and correct. I am most grateful to all of them: Debbie Bloomquist, Crystal Balyard, Eugenio Mely, Judy Fore, Michael Fore, Joseph Fuller, Lou and Dorie Kleis, Tony Gargiulo, Herminia Grant, William Grant, Art Kleinhesselink, Wayne Morales, Guy Palmer, James Rasmusser, Lucy Silva, Manny Silva, Stella Skeivik, Florence Kobuskie, Mary and Jennifer Ferris, Chaplains William Burke, James Boyd, Julian Gnall, Ken Kieffer, Joseph

LaMonde, and Kenneth Loughman.

A special note of thanks to Reverend Michael J. Wrenn of St. Joseph's Seminary, Dunwoodie, Yonkers, New York for reviewing the work and making many excellent suggestions.

The author is very grateful to the Most Reverend Leo T. Maher, D.D., Bishop of San Diego, for permission to work in the diocese during the writing of this book.

NOTE: The text uses the pronouns he, his, him, and often the nouns man and men in the generic sense as permitted by good English grammar to indicate any person, male or female, of the human family. Absolutely no discrimination or exclusion is intended.

On Using
My Bible

When I find a Bible reference at the end of a question, I should take time to look it up in my Bible. For example, when I see *Matthew 23.38,* I know that means the Gospel of St. Matthew, chapter 23, verse 38. Or when I see *1 John 4.16* I know that means the First Epistle of St. John, chapter 4, verse 16.

Sometimes the name of the book of the Bible is spelled out (for example, *Genesis*); at other times it may be shortened (as *Gen*). At the beginning of my Catholic Bible, I can find a list of all the books of the Bible and how these names are shortened, or abbreviated.

Looking up these references will not

only help me to understand the answers better but will also make me more acquainted with the Bible.

Also, in the notes at the beginning and end of my Catholic Bible, I can learn something about the history of the Bible and how the Church determined which writings were inspired by God and, therefore, to be included in the Bible.

CONTENTS

Preface

MILITARY ARCHDIOCESE
962 Wayne Avenue
Silver Spring, MD 20910

Office of the Archbishop
May 10, 1985

To all the faithful of the Military Archdiocese:

To have a practical knowledge of the faith and its scriptural foundation is important for every Catholic in today's world. It is even more important for a Catholic in the armed forces where the support of a Catholic community is not always available and where the faith is often challenged by very tempting behavioral opportunities and sometimes by criticism. In order to meet these challenges you need to review the facts of your faith as an adult and not rely on what you have learned as a child in the religious instructions of your early years.

Unfortunately, the shortage of Catholic chaplains makes it impossible to have adult religious education courses in the Catholic faith at every military facility. There has long been a need for a brief, concise, and very readable book that will present the basic teachings of the Catholic Church in such a way that you can review the facts of your faith with or without a teacher. I believe that this little book will, for the present, meet this need. *For this reason I strongly recommend that Catholic chaplains in the armed forces and the Veterans Administration make every effort to put this little book into the hands of as many personnel as possible.* While it is written primarily for young adults, this book can be very helpful to all Catholics interested in refreshing and renewing their grasp of the fundamentals of our Catholic faith.

My prayers and blessings go with this recommendation as do my expressions of gratitude for the tireless and self-sacrificing work the Catholic chaplains are doing for the men and women who are so courageously serving their nation.

Faithfully yours in Christ,

✝ Joseph T. Ryan
Archbishop of the
Military Archdiocese

Foreword

When young men and women enter the military service, they undergo what is known as "basic training," often followed by a period of technical training. During this time of indoctrination and early training, these young persons are inclined to take a new and more mature look at other values in life. For many it is a time to review and reevaluate religious ideals. For young Catholics it is a time to take a mature look at the teachings of the Church in which they have grown up. As young members of the military service face their new way of life, they often look for something in religion that will give them more than just memories from childhood. They are looking for something that will offer them a more meaningful way of life for adulthood. This little book is aimed at meeting this need at least in part.

A thoughtful reading of these pages will give young Catholics a quick review of their Catholic faith and the opportunity to realize now that the faith in which they grew up makes a great deal of sense in meeting the questions and problems of their young adult life.

You may recognize the questions, not as those you remember from your childhood religion classes, but as questions you may be asking yourself *now*! That's because these questions were actually asked by young adults like yourself. And because they were answered in cooperation with a group of young military personnel, you may find that the answers make a lot of sense in the struggle to get a grip on the meaning of life and love.

As a former Navy Chaplain myself, I believe this little book will meet your need for a short review of your faith as a young adult. I pray that your reading of these pages may be the occasion for a courageous turn in the direction of a more mature Christian personality as you become a more informed young Catholic who, as an adult, will own your faith and with pride and conviction profess and share it with others!

✝John Cardinal O'Connor, D.D., Ph.D.
Archbishop of New York

Introduction

Does This Sound Like Me?

I believe in God, and I still call myself a Catholic, but when I was a kid my parents *made* me go to Mass; they *made* me go to Confession; they *made* me go to catechism class . . . and frankly, I got pretty fed up with the whole thing. Now that I am grown up and in the service, I don't believe I have to do any of that stuff unless I feel like it!

That's right! Religion for a kid and religion for an adult are almost two different things. That's because children and adults are obviously quite different! Children do what they *feel* like doing unless their parents or someone in charge of them *makes* them do what they *ought* to do. Mature adults see the value in certain things and do what they *ought* to do regardless of how they *feel*. Growing up is a process of learning values and training myself to make decisions on my own.

For example, when I was a kid, my mother *made* me brush my teeth. She *made* me wash behind my ears. She *made* me comb my hair. My dad *made* me eat vegetables. He *made* me cover my mouth when I yawned or coughed. I still do these things today, not because my mother or dad *make* me do them, but because I have grown up and learned that they are good for my health, for my getting along with people, and for looking my best.

If I never learned the value of these things, I could turn out to be pretty much of a social reject. But I learned their value and made them "my own." I do them now because they are part of being a mature, responsible adult.

The same thing is supposed to happen in religion, in my relation to God. When I was a kid, I was in training. I was often "forced" to do what I didn't *feel* like doing, such as being obedient, controlling my temper tantrums, going to Mass, learning my catechism, praying, going to Confession, or staying awake during the sermon.

If all went well, at about the age of fourteen or so, I would begin to realize the value of all these things and start doing them on my own. I would do them because they were the right thing to do. I would do them because they would make me a thinking, loving adult. But it doesn't necessarily happen that way! I can stop thinking and studying about my religion so that all I remember is that "as a kid somebody *made* me do those things." So instead of growing, I go backwards. Instead of recognizing the value of my religion and making it "my own," I give it up and go on doing (at least in religious matters) what I *feel* like doing.

If that's the way I am . . . or if for any other reason I need to look at my Catholic religion as an adult, then this little book will help me "catch up" on what I may have missed. It will help me find out how and why my Catholic religion "makes sense" for me *as an adult!*

Faith

1. What must I believe in to be a Catholic?

To be a Catholic, I must believe in:
- God.
- His Word (expressed in the Bible and tradition).
- The Trinity (God the Father, Son, and Holy Spirit).
- Creation.
- Jesus (the Son of God who became man).
- The Church (including the Mass and the sacraments).
- Heaven and hell (the result of how I choose to live and love).
- Myself.

1

But not necessarily in that order.

All the objects of faith are a mystery . . .even myself. Sometimes faith in God begins with faith in myself!

---

2. What is a mystery?

A mystery is anything beyond my human understanding. There are many things I do not understand but could if I tried (like nuclear physics or how a TV works). The mystery I'm talking about is something I cannot understand fully even if I try.

---

3. What is faith?

Faith is a gift from God expressed in my willingness to accept and believe a mystery because it has been revealed or told to me in some way by God.

---

4. Am I a mystery?

I surely am! I can understand a lot about me . . . but not all.
(Psalm 92.6-7)

5. What has God said about me that I can't understand?

Well, I can't completely understand that I am going to live forever. I can't understand how I am spirit and body: that I have a soul, that I was created by God for love. I can't completely understand how I am free to love God or not love him, and that I can show my love for God by loving my neighbor. In fact, I can't understand completely how or why I am free to believe in him or not believe in him. Yes, I am full of mysteries, and that's one of the reasons why I need faith in myself.

Faith in myself is my willingness to believe I am somebody important, somebody worthwhile! I believe I can be the kind of person I choose to be. And I can choose to be a thinking, loving person who can overcome any weakness or obstacle in finding happiness for myself and for others.

(Matthew 13.37-43; John 14.1-4; 1 Corinthians 15.50-58)

6. What has God said about himself?

First of all, God said he exists. There

3

are a number of ways that I can understand that God *ought* to exist, but nothing really forces me to believe . . . the way putting my finger into an electrical socket would prove to me that electricity exists.

God said he created the world, that he is the source of beauty and order in things, and that all love and power come from him. But most of all, God said, "I AM." He said he exists! When I express my willingness to accept him, then I begin to experience his presence, his love, and his help.

(Hebrews 1.1-2; Exodus 3.13-15)

---

7. What did God say about creation?

God said *that* he created the world as a support system for man, whom he created for love. (I must not be confused by the fact that man has "fouled up" the world God created. The world still belongs to mankind, and when the human race decides to use the world properly, it will prove to be the best possible world.)

(Genesis 1.26-30; Psalm 8.4-9; Judith 16.13-14)

8. How did God create the world?

All we know for sure is *that* God created the world out of nothing. That is, nothing existed before God created the world. The beautiful story of creation in the first book of the Bible was not meant to tell us *how* God created the world but only *that* he created the world. The Bible was not written to satisfy my curiosity but only to meet my needs. I need to know *that* God created the world. I don't need to know *how* he did it. (If I want to believe the story of creation in the Bible, that's okay. But there are some technical difficulties in taking it literally. But then, there are quite a few technical difficulties in the theory of evolution and other theories too.) I can believe any theory on the origin of the world I want to as long as it begins with God.

(Genesis 1.1—2.3)

9. What do I mean when I say "God created man for love"?

First, let me remember that love is *not* an emotion. Love is not "how I feel" about someone. Love is a decision. It is a decision to share. Love, as a decision to share, can turn on every emotion I have, but love itself is not an emotion. I always need to remember this when I talk about love.

God created me out of love to share with me his own divine life. Because love is a two-way street, I was created in God's own image and likeness so that I could love God in return. I have the ability to know God and the ability to choose to love God so that I can decide to share *my* life with him.

(John 3.16-17; 1 John 4.16; Genesis 1.26; Romans 8.28-39)

---

10. Wait a minute! I'm getting lost. Did God love anyone before he created man?

Yes, but that is *the* number one mystery. I know it only because God said so. There is no way I can even begin to understand it. *Here* it is. God revealed himself as three persons in one God: the Father, the Son, and the Holy Spirit. We call this the TRINITY. I do not know *how* nor can I understand *how* there can be three persons in one God. All I know is *that* there are three persons in one God and *that* these three persons have loved each other so perfectly from all eternity that, really, I can say God is love!

(1 John 4.7-16; Matthew 28.19; Acts 2.33; 1 Corinthians 12.4-6; Romans 8)

---

11. Who is the Holy Spirit?

The Holy Spirit is the third person of the Blessed Trinity. The Holy Spirit together with the Father and the Son make up the one, true God. We know about God the Father from the story of creation and the coming of Jesus. We hear quite a bit about God the Son because it is he who became man in the person of Jesus. The Holy Spirit is the divine Spirit of truth, of love, and of life, whom Jesus promised to send into the world after he returned to the Father. While I am praying or studying my religion, the Holy Spirit reminds me of all the things that Jesus taught when he was on earth. The Holy Spirit helps me enjoy what I can understand and helps me accept what I cannot understand. The Holy Spirit also enables me to deal with the other ''spirits' in my life, like the spirit of selfishness, the spirit of

laziness, the spirit of false pride, the spirit of jealousy, and all the spirits of evil. I certainly want to strike up a prayerful friendship with God the Holy Spirit.
(Luke 3.21-22; Acts 2.1-4)

---

12. Just how, when, and where does God do this "revealing?"

During the first few thousand years of mankind's existence (just how many years is almost anyone's guess), the truth about God was passed on by the patriarchs, who were the grandfathers and great grandfathers of the families. The grandmothers surely had a big hand in it too. When the world population became larger, God designated prophets to reveal himself and his will to mankind. (Eventually, some of the work and words of the patriarchs and prophets were written down in what we now call the Old Testament of the Bible.) Finally, God sent his own divine Son into the world in the person of Jesus who gave us the clearest and most complete revelation about God: how God loves us and how we are to love him in return. In order to preserve and pass on the truth about God, his love, and his will for mankind, Jesus established his Church. (Some of the work and words of Jesus and his early disciples were eventually written down in what we now call the New Testament of the Bible.)

(John 21.25; Romans 1.18-20; Hebrews 1.1-3; Acts 8.26-39)

---

13. Tell me more about Jesus.

Jesus is the "second great mystery," not quite as far beyond my understanding as the Trinity, however. Let me go back a moment to the definition of love. Love is a decision to share. God loves us (mankind) so much that he shares his divine life with us. We were created to love God, so we (all of mankind) share human life with God. Jesus is that union of love between God and mankind. That union is the heart of the mystery. I cannot understand *how* God and mankind can be united in the one person of Jesus. But I know *that* God and mankind are truly united in Jesus because the prophets said it would happen and because Jesus, through his teaching and his works, showed us that he was both divine and human, both God and man.

Jesus had a better ID card than my little green card. His whole life was his ID card because he fulfilled every requirement and prediction made by the prophets, from being born of the Family of David in Bethlehem to dying on the cross for the salvation of mankind.
(John 1.1-3; Mark 9.7)

14. When did God and mankind become united in the person of Jesus?

Historically, it happened when a messenger from God announced to a young lady named Mary that, if she were willing, she would, by the power of the Holy Spirit, become the mother of the Messiah, the Son of God. Mary said yes, and as foretold by the prophet Isaiah, the Son of God was born of the Virgin Mary and was given the name Jesus. This happened about 2000 years ago in Israel. I can read the whole story in the Gospels, which are found in the first part of the New Testament in the Bible. (We celebrate Jesus' birthday on Christmas.)

15. If God created me and wants me to love him, why doesn't he just force me to

love him or create me in such a way that
I "have" to believe?

The quickest way to learn the answer
to that question is for me to walk up to
my girl friend and say, "You *have* to
love me." Or to my boyfriend and say,
"You *have* to believe me." I can find a
less violent answer if I remember that
faith is the "willingness" to believe and
that *love* is a "decision." Both are based
on the freedom not to believe or not to
love. Any force would reduce faith and
love to mere instinct.

16. What if I decide I don't want any religion? Maybe I'll be an atheist?

I can make any decision I want to.
However, whatever I decide, *that* is my
religion. My religion is whatever relation
I want to have with God. Either it is true
religion if I relate to him the way God
wants me to, or it is an invented religion
when I reject him in part. The atheist's
religion is total rejection. But acceptance
or rejection, believing or not believing,
does not affect the truth about God's existence or his love. It affects only *me*.

The Ten Commandments

17. **Why did God give mankind Ten Commandments?**

God gave mankind Ten Commandments for the same reason there are road signs and guardrails along the highway — to help me get where I want to go. Since God created me for love, he knows I really want to love him. But the going can get rough, and often I'm tempted not to love him. So God gave me some basic things to do and some basic things *not* to do in order to make sure I am really loving him and my neighbor.

18. **What are the Ten Commandments?**

They are recorded in the Bible in the book of Deuteronomy, chapter 5, verses 6 to 21. Briefly they are:

1. I, the Lord, am your God. Do not worship false gods.
2. You shall not take the name of the Lord, your God, in vain.
3. Remember to keep holy the sabbath day.
4. Honor your father and your mother.
5. You shall not kill.
6. You shall not commit adultery.
7. You shall not steal.
8. You shall not tell lies.
9. You shall not covet (desire) your neighbor's wife.
10. You shall not covet (desire) your neighbor's house or anything that belongs to him.

---

19. What do the Ten Commandments mean for me today?

Let me rewrite the Ten Commandments in terms of the situations in which I may find myself today.

1. I, the Lord, am your God. Do not worship money or any other possession or sensuous pleasure that might keep you

away from expressing love for your God. That includes your motorcycle, your sports car, and your luxury van. Beware of any religious fad that appeals to your emotions but ignores the one true God and his Son, Jesus. Don't be fooled by false messiahs and false prophets.

2. Do not use my name to describe everything that breaks or fails to work. Remember my last name is *not* damn.

3. In the Christian community, the Sabbath is Sunday. The least you can do to keep it holy is to participate in the Mass and avoid unnecessary hard work.

4. Be thoughtful of your parents and write to them *regularly* about your life in the service. They deserve it.

5. Do not kill unjustly (that includes murder, abortion, and suicide), and it also means avoiding any kind of harm to others or to yourself by physical violence or the abuse of drugs or alcohol.

6. Do not destroy your love power through the abuse of sex. Physical sex is the language of love for the exclusive use between a man and a woman united in marriage.

7. Respect the property of others and do not take anything or destroy anything

to which you have no right of ownership. This includes respect for government property.

8. Don't be a phony. Face the truth, speak the truth, act the truth. Especially, don't lie to yourself.

9. Don't let your imagination run wild and daydream about sex. The first step in controlling your actions is to control your thoughts.

10. Don't be envious of another's good fortune. You can't solve your problems by wishing you were someone else.

---

20. So, if I keep the Ten Commandments, does that make me a Catholic?

No, not really. But if I keep the Ten Commandments I *am* headed in the right direction. To be a Catholic means that I am a follower of Jesus Christ. The name *Catholic* was given to Christians in the second century. The word *catholic* means "universal" and was given to the Christians because by that time they were living their religion throughout most of the known world.

To Be a Christian

21. Then what do I need to do to be a Catholic, a Christian, a follower of Jesus Christ?

To answer that question in his own day and for all times, Jesus took a small group of his early followers called Apostles and started his Church. The Church is made up of people who want to follow Jesus under the leadership of the Apostles and the men who took the place of the Apostles. Today these men are called bishops, and as successors of the Apostles, they work in union with and under the leadership of the pope, the Bishop of Rome, the successor of St. Peter, and the Vicar (chief representative) of Jesus

16

Christ. But first, to be a Christian, I need
to know more about Jesus Christ himself.

22. What more do I need to know about Jesus?

Well, how much do I know about him
now? I remember from the story of
Christmas that he was born in Bethlehem
and his mother's name was Mary. Then
on Friday before Easter, he was
crucified, and on Easter Sunday, he rose
from the dead.

23. That's not much is it? What happened between the birth of Jesus and his death on the cross?

I guess I could pick up my Bible and
read the whole story in the Gospels.
There I would find that Jesus lived for
thirty-three years. He spent most of
those years at home in Nazareth working
as a carpenter to support himself and his
mother, Mary. (Apparently Joseph, the
foster father of Jesus, had died when
Jesus was a teenager.) At the age of thir-
ty, Jesus was introduced to the public by
his cousin, John the Baptizer. During the

next three years, Jesus identified himself as the Son of God, the Messiah. The word *Messiah* means the "anointed one" who was sent by God to save mankind. Jesus gave many signs, or proofs, of his identity in the form of miracles and by the wisdom of his teaching. The miracles of Jesus were not a magic show to entertain or a display of God's power to force anyone to believe. The miracles of Jesus included curing the sick, raising the dead, displaying power over nature, and foretelling a number of things, including his own death and resurrection, and the spread of his Church throughout the world.

But most of all, Jesus identified himself as the Son of God in his teaching about life and love. His death on the cross and his resurrection were the greatest lessons in what life and love are all about. But his words were power-packed and to the point as well. The people of his time said about Jesus, "No one ever spoke as he did." In teaching how to live and love and be happy, Jesus showed himself to be one with the Father and the Holy Spirit. His wisdom and knowledge about mankind showed that Jesus was there in the beginning when man was created. That's why I can believe what Jesus taught even though sometimes I do not understand everything he said. The first chance I get, I really ought to go back and read the whole story, especially the things Jesus taught in the Gospels about life and love. It's beginning to make a lot of sense! *(John 14.10; John 2.18-22; Matthew 7.28-29; Matthew 12.38-40)*

24. As a Catholic, what must I believe about Jesus?

As a Catholic, I must believe that Jesus is the Son of God made man, that he was born of the Virgin Mary, that he suffered and died for my sins, and that on the third day, he rose from the dead. After being with his Apostles and many of his other followers for a while after his resurrection, Jesus returned to the Father in heaven. He sent the Holy Spirit to be with the people of God in his Church and to help me and all Christians to remember and live what Jesus had taught. *(John 14.1-21)*

25. Just what did Jesus "save" me from?

In the first book of the Bible (Genesis), I can read the story of Adam and Eve. The story tells me that in the beginning mankind was given an opportunity to choose to love God or to choose *not* to love him. Out of pride and the selfish desire to be "like God," mankind, in the persons of Adam and Eve, chose *not* to love God, but to please itself. In this act of selfishness and disobedience, the first man and woman rejected God and lost their inheritance as children of God. They were no longer heirs to the eternal life in heaven. This failure to love by the first man and woman is known as *original sin*. Through this original sin, all mankind lost its inheritance to share in God's life in heaven. Jesus, as the Son of God, restored that inheritance to mankind and gave to me, as an individual, the opportunity to choose to love God and share in his life forever. I am reinstated as a child of God and heir to heaven through the Sacrament of Baptism.

I must remember, however, that I can lose that inheritance again through personal sin. I can lose heaven by personally choosing not to love, obey, and serve God. That's what I do when I live in very grave sin.

(Genesis 3.1-20; Romans 8.14-17)

---

26. Where does the Church come into the picture?

Jesus did not come into the world just for the people of the first century, nor just for the people of Israel. He came for all people of all time, but he had to start somewhere. Starting in Israel was no accident. Centuries before Jesus was born, the world had gotten so confused about God and the meaning of life that God made a deal, a covenant, with a man named Abraham. If Abraham and his family would be faithful to the one true God and the promise of a Messiah, his family would become, in a special way, "God's chosen people." This would occur even though the Messiah would come for all people of all nations. The chosen people had their ups and downs during the next couple thousand years. But they *did* succeed in maintaining belief in the one true God until the coming of the Messiah

in the person of Jesus. During all that
time, the prophets kept reminding the
chosen people about the one, true God.
They described in many ways what the
Messiah would be like when he came.
Jesus personally fulfilled everything the
prophets had said about the Messiah. To
fulfill the prophecy that the mission of
the Messiah would be to all nations and
for all future generations of people and to
make sure the truth about himself, about
life, and about love would be passed on,
Jesus started his Church.

*(Genesis 12.1-3; Jeremiah 31.31-34;
Matthew 2.1-6; Micah 5.2; Acts
7.1-53)*

---

27. How did Jesus start the Church?

Jesus started teaching in the northern
part of Israel called Galilee. He began by
talking with people and telling them that
the time had come for the fulfillment of
the prophecies about the Messiah. The
people were spellbound by his teaching
because he taught as one having authority. He sounded as if he really knew what
he was talking about. Jesus invited several Galilean men to become his disciples.

These twelve men stayed with Jesus for the next three years and listened to everything he taught. They watched the miracles he performed in proof of his words. Toward the end of the three years, Jesus indicated that Peter would be the head of the Apostles. Jesus said, "You are 'Rock,' and on this rock I will build my Church" (Matthew 16.18). The name Peter means rock. After his death and resurrection, Jesus singled out Peter again to be the leader of his Church. As Jesus promised, the Holy Spirit came to the Apostles on the first Pentecost. Under the leadership of Peter, they began to teach people about Jesus. The original Apostles were joined by other men like Matthias, Paul, Mark, Luke, Timothy, Barnabas, and others. Soon they were going to most of the known world telling people about Jesus and his teachings. Toward the end of the first century, the people who believed in Jesus began to be called Christians and were identified by the name of the town where they lived, for instance, *the Church at Corinth,* or *the Church at Macedonia,* or *the Church at Rome.* When the Apostles couldn't get to these places, they would write letters. Eventually four of these leaders of the Church wrote the story of Jesus and his teachings in what we call today the four Gospels. These letters and the four Gospels together with a little history of what the Apostles did during the years after Jesus died are what we call the New Testament in the Bible.

(Matthew 16.18-19; 28.18-20; John 10.14-16; Luke 22.32)

---

28. What about the Church today?

The Church today is doing basically the same things the Church did in the first century. The Church is made up of people like me who believe in Jesus as the Son of God. We practice our faith under the leadership of the successors of the Apostles whom we now call bishops. These bishops are assisted by priests and deacons. I remember that Jesus appointed Peter as head of the Apostles. Peter became the first pope as the Bishop of Rome, and his successors became the head of all the bishops and of the whole Church. From the earliest centuries, the Bishop of Rome has been called the pope, the Vicar (chief representative) of Jesus

Christ. Today the pope, the bishops, and the deacons study and pray about Jesus and his teachings so they in turn can teach other people the truth about Jesus and, through the sacraments, bring to all people the life and love that Jesus brought into the world.

But I have to be careful not to get the idea that we who are not bishops or priests have nothing to do in the Church. From the very beginning, we (who are called the laity) have held vital roles in the mission of the Church as Christian leaders in the social, commercial, and academic world. Today the need for such leadership is more important than ever! (*Matthew 24.14; 28.20; 1 Corinthians 12.1-31*)

One more thing about the Church. I must never forget the important and indispensable part that women have played in the origin, the history, and the success of the Church. What Jesus said to St. John at the foot of the cross, he said to the whole Church for all times. I remember how Jesus looked down from the cross and saw his mother, Mary, standing there with St. John. Almost like a last will and testament, Jesus said to St.

John, "There is your mother!" (John 19.25-27). From that day on, Mary, the mother of Jesus, became the mother of all who would follow Jesus in his Church. And through Mary, all Christian women were destined to become spiritual mothers of the Church as they cultivate, nourish, and protect the living faith among the followers of Jesus. This role of spiritual motherhood is something that no one else can ever fill. Whether it be in the smaller, sublime circle of the family, in the secular career of the unmarried, or as a consecrated member of a religious community where they experience spiritual motherhood for literally thousands, Christian women have always played the vital and irreplaceable role of spiritual motherhood in the family of God, which we call the Church.

The Sacraments

29. What are the sacraments?

I've heard some Christians talk about being born again. Well, the sacraments give me the opportunity not only to be born again in the Spirit of Jesus, but to grow up again in the life of Jesus. There are seven sacraments. They cover my whole lifetime, especially the most important moments in my life.
(Romans 6.3-6)

30. Just what is a sacrament?

When talking about the seven sacraments, I define a sacrament as an outward sign instituted by Jesus Christ to give grace. (They are the very actions of Christ that give us a share in his divine life and change us in various ways if our hearts are open to him.) I see there are three important parts to each one of the seven sacraments. First, there is an outward sign that means there is something I can see, feel, or hear. Second, it was instituted by Jesus Christ. There are many other signs or sacraments in the Church, which we usually call sacramentals, such as the sign of the cross, blessings, holy water, and the crucifix. They are outward signs, but they were not instituted by Jesus. Third, a sacrament gives grace. That means the sacrament actually gives me a share in God's life, his love, and his presence in my life.

31. What are the names of the seven sacraments?

The seven sacraments are Baptism, Confirmation, the Eucharist, Penance, Matrimony, Holy Orders, and the Anointing of the Sick.

32. How do the seven sacraments line up with my natural life?

It will be easier to see how they relate to my natural life if I compare the following two lists point by point.

My Natural Life

• When I was born, I received human life from my parents.

• When I grow up, I become an adult member of the human family, responsible for the preservation and defense of human rights and human dignity.

• When I eat properly, I cultivate my human life and keep healthy.

• When I injure my body or lessen my human life in sickness, I go to a doctor and take medicine to get cured.

• When I decide to get married, I do some serious thinking about how my spouse and I can unite our lives in love and how we can become responsible parents.

• When I decide to become a priest, I am choosing to invest my whole life in the service of others.

• When I am critically or terminally ill, I need courage and patience as well as medicine to help me through those final hours.

The Seven Sacraments

• When I receive the Sacrament of Baptism, I receive divine life from God.

• When I receive the Sacrament of Confirmation, I receive the Holy Spirit in a special way to help me become a mature member of the Christian community, responsible for the preservation and defense of Christian truth about life and love.

• When I worthily receive the Body and Blood of Jesus in the Holy Eucharist (Holy Communion), I cultivate the life and love of God in me.

• When I lessen or destroy the life of God in me by sinning, I receive the Sacrament of Penance (also called Confession or

Sacrament of Reconciliation) with forgiveness from Jesus and a new chance to share his life and love.

• When I get married, I receive the Sacrament of Matrimony in which I am given added grace enabling me to share my whole life, both physical and spiritual, with my spouse and meet the responsibilities of parenthood.

• When I receive the Sacrament of Holy Orders, I am given a special share in God's life and love as well as the power to administer the sacraments to others.

• When I am critically ill, I receive the Sacrament of the Anointing of the Sick in which I receive not only forgiveness for my sins but also a new surge of divine life and love that can help me get well or help me through those final hours.

Baptism and Confirmation

33. How was I baptized?

I was born into a Catholic family, so a couple of weeks after I was born, my parents took me to the church where the priest, in a very beautiful ceremony, poured water over my head and said: "I baptize you in the name of the Father, and of the Son, and of the Holy Spirit." This is what Jesus told the Apostles to do. Some people who become Catholics later in life go through much the same ceremony after a series of classes and a process of Christian initiation usually lasting several months.

(John 3.5; Matthew 28.18-20; Romans 8.14-17; 2 Corinthians 5.17)

34. I remember receiving the Sacrament of Confirmation when I was about seven or eight years old. My friend says he doesn't remember ever being confirmed. Can he still receive the Sacrament of Confirmation?

In the very early days of the Church, it was mostly adults who were baptized, became Christians, and received the Holy Spirit in the Sacrament of Confirmation. There is mention of "entire families" being baptized, so I guess some infants were baptized and received Confirmation too. (See Acts 16.15.) But mostly, it was a matter that concerned adults. That's why the Sacrament of Confirmation was received at the time of or shortly after Baptism.

In various parts of the world, Confirmation is given at different times, mostly depending on the availability of the bishop. In some places, Confirmation is delayed until a person is in the middle or late teens and after a year or two of special instruction. So, yes, my friend can still receive the Sacrament of Confirmation, and I ought to exercise *my* grace of Confirmation by taking my friend to the instruction classes both to help him and to refresh my own knowledge and faith. (I can check with the Catholic chaplain about the time and place for the instructions.)

35. How is the Sacrament of Confirmation given?

Ordinarily, a bishop administers the Sacrament of Confirmation. First, he extends his hands over me (just as the Apostles did) and prays:

"All-powerful God, Father of our Lord Jesus Christ, by water and the Holy Spirit you freed your sons and daughters from sin and gave them new life. Send your Holy Spirit upon them to be their Helper and Guide. Give them the spirit of wisdom and understanding, the spirit of right judgment and courage, the spirit of knowledge and reverence. Fill them with the spirit of wonder and awe in your presence. We ask this through Christ our Lord. Amen."

After I renew my baptismal promises, the bishop anoints me with blessed oil

saying, "Be sealed with the Gift of the Holy Spirit."
(Acts 8.5-17)

36. What does Confirmation do for me?

Just as "growing up" is the fulfillment of what happened when I was born, so Confirmation is the fulfillment of what happened at my Baptism when I first received divine life. In Confirmation, I receive the Holy Spirit again but in a stronger way. With his help, I am able to live my faith more fully and share it more lovingly and courageously. With Confirmation, I receive the grace to become a responsible member of the Christian community, making every effort to live a healthy, happy Christian life and to share that health and happiness with others.
(Luke 12.11-12; Matthew 5.14-16; 10.32-33)

The Holy Eucharist, Mass, and Communion

37. I can remember how I used to receive Holy Communion, and I seemed to get so much out of it. Now, well . . . I don't know.

As they say in the Navy, "Perhaps I lost the bubble!" It may be that I forgot what Holy Communion is really all about. Perhaps I started neglecting my faith, so that Holy Communion could have little or no effect on my life. It happens in my physical life the same way. I may eat good food at mealtime, but in between, I fill myself with so much junk that the good food cannot offset the bad food. I get sick or weak, even though I may *look* healthy.

38. What is Holy Communion really all about?

It's really all about love and love power. Briefly, here's what happened. It was Thursday evening, the day before Jesus died on the cross. Jesus was with his Apostles having a special supper to celebrate the Jewish feast of the Passover. (That's the feast remembering the escape of the Jewish people from Egypt.) At this supper, Jesus gave the Apostles a final briefing and a farewell talk in which he told them that he did not want to leave them alone because he loved them so much. Jesus took a piece of bread, broke it into pieces and said, "Take this, all of you and eat it: this is my body." And taking a cup of wine, he gave thanks and passed it to them to drink, saying, "This is the cup of my blood. . . . It will be shed for you and for all so that sins may be forgiven. Do this in memory of me."

Jesus took the two most common foods in the world and changed them into his Body and Blood to be the food of my soul and the nourishment of the divine life that I received in baptism. He left the world in his visible form so as not to force me to believe in him. ("Blest are they who have not seen and have believed," Jesus told the Apostles. See John 20.29.) But Jesus remains with me in this sacrament of love so that I might continue to receive from him an abundance of life and love, as well as the power to love others. In Holy Communion, I receive the Body and Blood of the living Jesus under the appearances of bread and wine. It is in union with Jesus that I can really live, love, and find happiness. *(Matthew 26.26-28; Mark 14.22-24; 1 Corinthians 11.24-31)*

---

39. Jesus said, "Do this in memory of me." How do I do that today?

The phrase, "Do this in memory of me" means more than just "to remember." It means to "relive". . . to re-present the whole scene including the Last Supper on Holy Thursday, the death of Jesus on the cross on Good Friday, and his resurrection on Easter Sunday. This reliving takes place in the Holy Sacrifice of the Mass. In the Mass, Jesus, acting through the priest, again changes bread and wine into his Body and Blood. Jesus offers himself to God the Father as my risen Savior. The living Jesus is really and truly present under the appearances of bread and wine in the Holy Eucharist. That's why I make a sign of respect by kneeling or bowing when I enter or leave the church. And that's why I act respectfully during Mass.

I participate in the Mass by listening to the words of Jesus, by uniting myself with Jesus in Holy Communion, by offering myself with Jesus to the Father in a sacrifice of love, and by praying that I might one day be united with Jesus in the glory of heaven.

40. How do I learn more about the Mass?

Probably the best way to learn more about anything is to experience it. Sure, to read and study *about* the Mass is good (and there are many books written about the Mass). But to go with others and participate in the Mass is even better. There I can see how the Mass has two big parts, one for prayerful instructions, the other for prayerful worship. The first part is called the Liturgy of the Word, and the other is called the Liturgy of the Eucharist.

The Liturgy of the Word includes an introduction in which I join with others in expressing sorrow for sin, sorrow for having failed to love the way I should. The priest offers a prayer for forgiveness. Grateful for God's mercy, everyone says or sings a song of praise that starts "Glory to God in the highest." After the priest says a prayer for all of us, I listen to readings from the Bible taken from both the Old Testament and the New Testament. The homily (sometimes called a sermon) is given by the priest or a deacon to explain the readings from the Bible and bring the Word of God into my life today. There's so much I can learn by listening carefully to the readings and to the homily.

In response to the Word of God, I stand up with the rest of the people and profess my faith by reciting the Nicene Creed in which I declare my belief in the three persons of the Blessed Trinity: God the Father as Creator, God the Son in the person of Jesus as my Savior and Redeemer, and God the Holy Spirit who sanctifies me and gives me life. I also profess my faith in the Word of God, as spoken by the prophets of old and by the Catholic Church today. I declare my belief in one baptism, the forgiveness of sins, and the resurrection of the dead into the life of the world to come.

After this profession of faith, I offer with the priest a prayer asking for God's help for myself and for others.

The second part of the Mass, the Liturgy of the Eucharist, begins with a prayer of thanks and the offering of the bread and wine. Now comes the heart of the Mass: the re-presenting of what Jesus did at the Last Supper. Bread and wine are changed into the Body and Blood of Jesus. I recognize the words from the Gospel, but I also notice that the priest does *not* say, "This is the body of Jesus," but he says, "This is *my* body . . . this is the cup of *my* blood." At that moment the priest is taking the place of Jesus. Jesus is acting *through* the priest, and I am actually reliving the scene at the Last Supper.

After saying or singing the Our Father with the rest of the congregation, I have the opportunity to receive into my heart the living Jesus under the appearances of bread and wine. (I can receive the living Jesus under the appearances of bread *or* wine *or* both.)

The final prayers of the Mass remind me that I have received Jesus and am now expected to go out and share him with others by my love and my example. *(John 6.47-59)*

41. How often should I receive Holy Communion?

I should receive Holy Communion every time I participate in the Mass, unless I have committed a serious sin, in which case I need to confess my sin first and receive the Sacrament of Penance (now frequently called Reconciliation).

Sacrament
of Penance
(Reconciliation)

42. I really don't like the idea of
confessing my sins!

That's two of us! In fact I don't know of
anyone who *likes* to admit doing wrong.
It's not easy to face failure and plead
guilty. But I do like to correct my
mistakes. I also know that admitting an
error is the first step toward correcting
the error. Sometimes I think my big
problem is confessing my sins *to
myself!*

43. But why confess to a priest? I don't
remember anyone ever confessing sins to
Jesus!

That's right. No one confessed sins to Jesus the way I am asked to confess my sins to a priest. Sure, a couple of people like Zacchaeus and Mary Magdalene *admitted* their sins to Jesus, but they didn't have to because Jesus, as the Son of God, already knew the condition of their souls: their sins, their faith, their sorrow. I'm glad Jesus didn't give his priests *that* power. What Jesus *did* give his priests was the power to forgive me my sins after I reveal my sins, my faith, and my sorrow.

Here's what happened. Shortly after his resurrection, Jesus came to the Apostles and said, "Receive the Holy Spirit. If you forgive men's sins, they are forgiven them; if you hold them bound, they are held bound" (John 20.23).

There's no doubt that the Apostles received the power to forgive sins. But they were also told to make a decision. Does the person's sorrow and faith make forgiveness possible? Only after a person reveals the state of his soul is the priest able to make that decision. In the very early centuries, this "revealing," or confessing, was done *publicly*. That didn't last long. Later, the confessing was done in private. Eventually small rooms or confessionals were used.

Anyway, I confess my sins to the priest so that he can decide whether I am truly open to receive God's forgiveness. But there are other reasons for confessing my sins too.

(John 8.3-11; Luke 15.7)

---

44. What are the other reasons for confessing my sins to the priest?

Besides receiving forgiveness for my sins, I find that going to Confession helps me to know myself better. Confession helps me to refine my love power so that I see the difference between clever self-ishness and true love. From the priest, I get some good tips on how to develop a mature and responsible personality. I learn how to get rid of destructive habits and cultivate habits that will bring me real happiness. Confession helps me *grow inside,* so that when I *look* like an adult I really *am* an adult.

But most of all, for me, Confession keeps me honest, so I don't kid myself along and think I am loving when I am not. It keeps me from *feeling* I am right when I am wrong. It keeps me from hurting those I love with my temper or my misunderstanding. I guess that's why Confession is sometimes called the Sacrament of Reconciliation. It reconciles me, or restores me, to a loving relationship with God, with others, and with my real self.

(2 Corinthians 5.15-20)

---

45. Is there a special "form" or "way" that I should go to Confession?

The usual form for going to Confession is helpful but not absolutely necessary. However, certain things *are* necessary for me to do in order to make a good Confession.

- I need to examine my conscience.
- I need to mention how long it has been since my last Confession.
- I need to mention *all* my serious sins.
- I need to make a good act of contrition.
- I need to do whatever penance the priest gives me.

Examination of conscience: I need to look over the time since my last Confession to remember in what ways and how often I may have sinned. It may be

46

helpful to use the Ten Commandments in examining my conscience. (See questions 17, 18, and 19.)

Mention time of last Confession: This does not mean the date of my last Confession, but approximately how long it has been.

Mention all serious sins: I need to mention *all* the serious sins I can remember. If I am not sure whether something is a serious sin, I can simply tell the priest what I did and let him help me decide, so as to avoid the sin or the doubt in the future. If I honestly forget a serious sin and think of it later, I do not have to dash back to Confession. I need only to mention it in my next regular Confession. It is also good to mention some of my lesser, or venial, sins.

Make an act of contrition: This can be one I know by heart, or I can say in my own words that I am sorry for my sins and intend to make every effort to avoid them in the future.

Do the penance: The priest may give me several prayers to say or something else that may help me to deal with a problem or a habit I may have.

The Usual Form: (After entering the confessional I say:)

Bless me Father for I have sinned.

My last confession was . . . (three weeks, months, years) ago.

(It may be helpful to the priest if I also mention here how old I am and whether or not I am married.)

These are my sins. . . .

I am sorry for these and all the sins of my past.

(Here the priest will give me some helpful advice and then ask me to make an act of contrition.)

Act of Contrition: O My God, I am heartily sorry for having offended you. I detest all my sins, because I dread the loss of heaven and the pains of hell. But most of all, I am sorry because I have offended you who are worthy of all my love. I firmly resolve with the help of your grace to confess my sins, to do penance, and to amend my life. Amen.

A Little Different Form: (I like this one because I need to be constantly reminded that sin is the failure to love.)

Bless me Father. It has been (three weeks, months, years) since my last con-

48

fession. Here are the ways I have failed to love. (Some examples follow.)

- I failed to love my parents by being angry and disrespectful to them and ignoring their wishes.
- I failed to love myself by cheating in a test.
- I failed to love my neighbor by damaging his property.
- I failed to love my girl friend by touching her improperly for my own selfish pleasure.
- I failed to love myself and my neighbor by telling lies to justify my actions or make myself look better.

(After telling my sins, I say:)

"I am sorry for these and all the sins of my past. Now I really do want to love God, my neighbor, and myself."

(After the priest gives his advice and tells me what penance I should say or do, I make an act of contrition.)

Act of Contrition: Lord, I know I was created to love. I am sorry for having failed to love when I should have. Forgive me and let my life be filled with love for you, for my neighbor, and for myself. Amen.

46. Just what is sin?

When I was young, I was taught that sin meant breaking the law of God. And that's true. But as an adult, I can understand that the Ten Commandments (and all God's laws, given directly or through the Church) are aimed at helping me to love God, my neighbor, and myself. So, sin is really *the failure to love*. The Commandments tell me when I am or am not loving. In other words, the Commandments say, "When you honor your parents you are loving them. When you keep holy the Sabbath day you are loving God. When you steal, you are *not* loving. When you lie, you are *not* loving. When you abuse sex, you are *not* loving . . ." and so on through the Commandments and laws of the Church.

(Matthew 22.34-40; Romans 3.20)

47. How do I recognize a "serious" sin from a "venial" sin?

A sin is considered *serious,* or *mortal,* when it has to do with a serious matter (such as causing serious injury to someone, the abuse of sex, abortion, stealing a car, or publicly destroying someone's good name). Besides the serious matter, there must be my free consent after full deliberation. That means that no one is forcing me to do it. I am free *not* to do it. I *know* what I am doing, and I just don't care! I freely choose *not* to love God, my neighbor, or myself.

A *venial* sin has to do with a small matter, only partial consent, or a lack of total freedom in the matter.

---

48. How often should I go to Confession?

I should go to Confession regularly. That could mean every few weeks or every couple months, depending on myself and the condition of my life. I know the law says I *have* to go to Confession only when I have committed a serious sin. I guess it really depends on what I am trying to do. If I don't care what happens to my car, I don't have to check the oil until the motor starts to burn up. If I don't care what's happening to my life and my love power, I don't have to go to Confession until I really foul up. Again, as with my car, preventive maintenance is easier and smarter.

49. What's a rather common mistake I can make in going to Confession?

I think one of the most common mistakes is to think of Confession as a spiritual Laundromat in which I commit sin (fail to love), get washed up (go to Confession), and then go out carelessly and sin again. It just doesn't work that way! Unless I am determined to make every effort to avoid the sin in the future, my sins simply are *not* forgiven.

50. But what if I am not sure I can avoid the sin?

I'm never sure I can avoid the sin. But I *can* be sure I am going to try as hard as I can to avoid the sin. And that means avoiding the occasion of the sin. Hardly anyone wakes up in the morning saying, "I am going to sin today." Sin is like a freeway or a parkway. I can't get on it unless I get on the approach road. If I don't want to get on the freeway, I stay off the approach road. If I don't want to sin, I stay away from whatever leads up to the sin. When I know I am going to try as hard as I can to avoid sin, then I can make a good Confession, even if in the future my efforts fail and I sin again.

---

51. What if I'm ashamed to tell a sin?

I guess it's natural to be ashamed to tell certain sins. I just wish I were as ashamed to *commit* the sin as I am to confess it. However, if I am ashamed because I think the priest is going to be shocked or think less of me, I can forget that. Priests have heard it all. And because of the "seal of Confession," the priest cannot use what I say in Confession to even think, much less talk about it outside the confessional, not even to me!

But because I am ashamed sometimes, I make another mistake. I try to tell my sins in such a way that they do not sound so bad to myself or to the priest. Or sometimes I say things in general, like "I stole" or "I lied" or "I lost my temper" or "I was impure." If I don't try to be more specific, I can cheat myself out of the help the priest can give me to improve myself.

I am not kidding anyone but myself if I say in Confession, "I made love with a girl" when what I really did was "make selfishness with a girl." To be more exact, "I *used* a girl (or my girl friend) to satisfy my own selfish pleasure." When I am honest with myself like this, then I begin to realize that I have failed to love, and I might start thinking about acting differently, especially if I really *want* to love a particular girl. Only when I am honest can the priest help me restore and preserve my love power.

---

52. But I still don't like the idea of confessing my sins.

One of the great things I need to learn in growing up is that I don't have to *like* everything I do. In fact, one of the marks of real maturity is the ability to do what I know I *ought* to do even if I don't like it. As an adult, if I really am in charge of my own life, I often choose to do what I know I should do, in spite of the fact that I may not *like* it. That, by the way, is what they tried to teach me in boot camp.

---

53. Isn't God everywhere? So why do I need to go to church to pray? Why can't I confess my sins directly to God?

Yes, God is everywhere. But there are many ways for a person to be present. I will find that out when I get stationed somewhere far from home, far from the girl I love. Sure, she is present to me everywhere . . . in her picture on my locker door, in my dreams, in the letters she sends, in my mind when I go shopping for a gift, in the cookies she bakes and wraps so carefully, in the photo in my wallet. She's there when I gaze out at the sunset or look at the same moon she might be looking at. Yes, in many ways she's everywhere. But not the way she is at home when I am there with her. Believe me, there's a difference.

When the church is called "the house of God," that is not just a figure of speech. God *is* present there in a very special way in the Blessed Sacrament of the Eucharist. And being there with God in his eucharistic presence is like being at home with him. And that's special. That's different.

The same goes for confessing sins and obtaining forgiveness. I could tell the one I love that I am sorry for offending her in many ways. I could say it to her picture. I could say it in my dreams of her. I could say it when I'm thinking of her in the moonlight. But the only way I am going to get an answer of forgiveness and be *sure* I am back in her good graces is to tell her when and where she can give me an answer.

God has given me the Sacrament of Penance so that he can let me know I really am forgiven when he says through the priest, "Your sins are forgiven. Now go in peace" (Luke 7.48, 50). Come to think of it, confessing my sins in the Sacrament of Penance (or Reconciliation) is, in fact, confessing my sins directly to God. Didn't Jesus tell the Apostles, "He who hears you, hears me"? What more could I ask for?
(Luke 10.16)

54. Don't I have a right to follow my own conscience?

I surely do, provided I *have* a right and healthy conscience. My conscience is not my imagination. Nor is it some kind of automatic organ like the kidney or intestines that sort out the good and eliminate the waste matter. Rather, the conscience is a faculty like my intelligence or my love power that must be cultivated and developed according to truth and reality. My conscience can become paralyzed by sinful habits and emotional preferences. Like a paralyzed body that cannot feel pain, the paralyzed conscience cannot detect or recognize evil. And I cannot follow a paralyzed conscience! That's why it is important for me to develop a right and healthy conscience that has been correctly formed according to the teachings of Jesus and his Church.

Marriage,
Love,
Sex

55. Why is marriage a sacrament?

Marriage (Sacrament of Matrimony) is one of the seven sacraments because it is an important turning point in my life. I take on new responsibilities and need God's help to fulfill them. Marriage is not easy. True love is not easy. Being parents is not easy. Married couples know that. And God knows that too. That's why God offers married couples all the help they need to be successful in marriage by giving them the grace of the sacrament. Of course, to find happiness, married couples need to *use* the grace God gives them. (*Genesis 2.21-24; Ephesians 5.21-33; Mark 10.2-12*)

56. Why does marriage seem so difficult?

Marriage is not all that difficult *if* the couple really work at it and remember what marriage is all about. Marriage is the union of two *total* persons, not just two bodies. And true love is not "how they feel" about each other, but a *decision* on the part of both the man and the woman to share their total lives with each other. If their love for each other is no more than an emotion, no more than how they *feel* about each other, then all it takes to break up the marriage is a more intense feeling in another direction. That's why a fellow or a girl, after a few years of marriage, can come up with that strange statement, "I don't feel like being married anymore." It takes about forty-five minutes or less to *get* married. It takes at least seven years to *become* married. Becoming married means making everything work toward the union of two minds, two hearts, two emotional personalities, two inner selves, two spiritual persons . . . and giving expression to this total union in the thrilling pleasure of physical union. This physical expression of the total union of love is not only the most intensive physical pleasure but also the most creative power possessed by mankind — a power which enables a couple to bring into the world a new person as the fruit of love. This fulfilling and creative union of love is what marriage is all about.

---

57. Why does the Church seem to make it so difficult for me to get married?

The Church is primarily and intensely interested in my finding all the happiness that God intended for married couples. When I stop to think about it, I really appreciate the reasons why I, as a Catholic, can receive the Sacrament of Matrimony validly only in the presence of a Catholic priest. The Church wants to make sure I know what I am doing, that I truly *am* in love, that there is no obstacle to the marriage, and that I know how to use God's graces in making a success of my marriage. To do all that takes time, instruction, and some paperwork. But I find that's the case with any "insurance policy." And as in any insurance policy, I must remember to pay the premium, or the policy is no good. The premium for insuring success in marriage is the mature effort to eliminate selfishness and cultivate true love, which, I must remember, is the firm decision (renewable each day) to share myself totally with my spouse.

---

58. Why is the Church so strongly against birth control?

The Church is not against the control of the number of births in my family when that control is based on proper and sound reasons. The Church *is* against artificial birth prevention! I know the teaching authority in the Church exists to preserve the truth about God, life, and my eternal destiny, as well as to preserve true love in justice. Anything that threatens truth or love, the Church opposes.

It is an historical fact (and the evidence in the modern world is overwhelming) that when the male of the species (that means a "man") has unlimited access to physical sex, his use of physical sex strongly tends to deteriorate into a utilitarian appetite for selfish pleasure. That means he runs the risk of using his wife for selfish pleasure and thinking of her as little more than a source of tranquilizing satisfaction, rather than a companion in making love. Everyone *hates* to be used. In artificial birth prevention, that is exactly what can happen. Women risk being *used!* For convenience sake some women may not like to admit that, but eventually the truth surfaces, and a greater strain is put on the marriage than children ever cause.

There is a very good and reliable way of controlling the number of births. It is called the "Billings Ovulation Method" or the "Sympto-Thermal Method." It takes a little effort and planning. But so does true love.

---

59. Why do people get so excited over child abuse but argue passionately in favor of abortion?

If I could think of a real social mystery this would be it. Child abuse is such an obvious crime that no one can cover it over with excuses or fictitious arguments. The news media carry stories of child abuse bluntly, and they graphically portray the battered bodies of children in pictures so that the public is justifiably outraged.

Abortion, the killing of an unborn child in its mother's womb, is equally obvious as a crime, but it is covered over by calling the unborn child "nothing but a fetus" or "just fetal matter." Pro-abortion groups, calling themselves "pro-choice," try to make abortion sound like a personal right. They use tear-jerker stories about embarrassed or economically deprived mothers with unwanted children to promote abortion. Yet no one seems to know the origin of the right to make a choice between killing or not killing an unborn child. The news media treat abortion as if it were some kind of vaccine for a disease and refuse to publish the graphic pictures that show garbage cans full of the bodies of unborn children, some still breathing, others with tears running down their infant cheeks. That, they say, is getting emotional. Besides, it might disturb those in favor of abortion and cause the public to be outraged. It doesn't make sense, but that's what is happening. The Church condemns abortion because killing an unborn child not only breaks the Fifth Commandment, it shatters it!

---

60. What's wrong with premarital sexual intercourse?

First of all, premarital sex is a lie, no matter how intense the feeling might be. Physical sex is the language of love reserved exclusively for a man and a woman united in marriage. When married couples make love, that is exactly what they are doing. They are saying to each other in the nonverbal language of sexual intimacy that they have publicly, before God and human witnesses, declared their total commitment to each other, to share themselves without reservation, until death. To steal the pleasure without the commitment is a lie and an injustice.

And speaking of injustice, I can't help but think about the child who is often brought into the world this way. Such a child gets a raw deal and is shortchanged in terms of family, family love, and future. That's real injustice, especially when I consider that such a child's life is just as important as mine is — no more no less.

61. What difference does a little piece of paper, a marriage certificate, make? If it is all right two weeks "after" I get married, why is it wrong two weeks before?

It's the difference between having a right and not having a right. Try the same thing in the banking business. My rich uncle promises to give me twenty-thousand dollars on my twenty-first birthday. Two weeks before my birthday, I decide I want the money *now*. So I go over to the bank with a mask and gun and take the money, saying, "After all, in two weeks it will be mine." That's what I told the policeman when I got caught. Result: I am now charged with grand larceny.

Now the scene changes. Two weeks *after* my birthday I walk into the bank with a little piece of paper (called a check). I endorse the check and draw out twenty-thousand dollars. The bank manager says, "Nice doing business with you." The policeman smiles and waves good-bye. The *difference:* The "little piece of paper" gave me a *right* to the money; the mask and gun did not!

62. What's wrong with reading "skin" magazines?

The people in the computer business have a saying: "Garbage in, garbage out." If I fill my mind with ideas and pictures promoting the abuse of sex, I am going to find myself with little or no appreciation for the real meaning of sex and a strong tendency to abuse sex in my own life. It's not worth it! The publishers of skin magazines are doing as much harm to society as the dope peddlers are.

63. Just what harm does the abuse of sex cause me? And why is it a sin?

I'm talking here about moral harm to me as a person. (For a rundown on physical or legal harm, I can check with the medical and legal officers.) First I must recall that self-control in sex (called chastity) gets its importance from the relationship between sex and love. Love is the most important virtue in life and the greatest single source of happiness. (After love come faith and hope.) The abuse of sex lessens or destroys not only my love (and often my faith and my hope) but even worse. The abuse of sex can destroy my love power, my ability to love!

I can check it out with the troops. A fellow who engages for any length of time in all sorts of sex abuse every chance he gets ends up seeing a girl as nothing more than a toy for his own selfish pleasure. If he continues in that kind of behavior, he finds, one day when he meets the girl he really *wants* to love, that he simply doesn't have any love power. He is not able to love her. He can only use her as a toy for his own selfish pleasure. I cannot love a "thing"; I can love only a person. If because of my addiction to sex abuse, I cannot see beyond the "wrappings," if I cannot see the *person* in the girl I want to love, then I will never be able to love her until I restore my love power. I will only be able to "use" her for my own selfish pleasure. And that's pretty sad.

When I hear a group of the guys talking about girls, it is interesting to hear how they describe them. Try it. It seems many of them can no longer see a person to love, but only a set of measurements to drool over. The sad thing is that it works the same way with girls who are involved in sex abuse.

One thing's for sure. If my ability to love is the price I pay for sex abuse, it's a stupid and lousy trade-off.

The abuse of sex can also destroy my faith. I can find myself throwing away that gift of faith when my religion stands in the way and will not support my addiction to sex abuse.

In trying to feed my addiction to sex abuse, I can also find myself turning against my parents and rejecting their love and caring advice in favor of some strangers who couldn't care less about my love power, my faith, or my future happiness.

Sex abuse is a sin because it attacks and can destroy just about everything I was created to be, my love, my maturity, my faith in God, and my faith in myself. (1 Corinthians 6.9-11)

A confusing example of sex abuse today is the practice of homosexuality. This is not something new. According to the drawings on the walls of ancient Pompeii in Italy, the practice of homosexuality existed rather widely during the declining years of the Roman Empire. Even long before that, Moses found it necessary to condemn the practice of homosexuality in very strong words. (See Leviticus 20.13.) What is relatively new today is the effort to justify the practice of homosexuality as a normal use of a person's sexuality.

In considering the matter of homosexuality, I need to remember that my sexuality is *not* a simple matter. Just as the use of my ability to think correctly, to make right decisions, and to enjoy reality fully takes some training or at least some common sense, the proper use of my sexuality requires some education, self-control, and good common sense.

I know that the primary purpose of my sexuality is to communicate creative love to my partner in marriage. But because the use of my sexuality involves such intense, emotional and physical pleasure that can be experienced in almost any physical contact, I can easily lose sight of this primary purpose and find myself using my sexuality in search of no more than the pleasure. And because the self-satisfying pursuit of sexual pleasure can be so addictive, I can easily make mistakes and cleverly try to justify these mistakes in the abuse of my sexuality. One such mistake is to confuse the desire for sexual pleasure with love. Another mistake is saying that sexual pleasure has no more purpose than pleasure itself. Some people may admit the primary purpose but also insist that my sexuality has a secondary purpose of pleasure to be obtained any way I can get it. That's why the abuses of sexuality such as adultery, fornication, homosexual practices, and masturbation are regarded by some as no more than "sexual preferences."

There is no doubt that some psychological dimensions do exist in the problem of homosexuality, and I certainly ought to have a caring respect for the person who is struggling with this problem. At the same time, I must be careful not to try to justify homosexual actions by confusing the *condition* of homosexuality with homosexual *practices*. Homosexuality is a tendency and a temptation. Homosexual practice is a sinful abuse of sexuality.

---

64. Then what is the value of chastity?

Chastity is one of the major ways to develop and practice self-control. Self-control is what puts me in charge of my own life so that I can be truly free from addictions of any sort and free to *choose* to be who I ought to be — a mature, thinking, loving person.

Most of all, chastity protects my ability to love people unselfishly and generously; chastity also increases my world of pleasure so that I have a greater capacity to enjoy the world of nature, music, movies, art, travel, and just about everything, because I do not narrow everything down to sex pleasure or the demand for sex-abuse opportunities.

Chastity is not a binding force but a liberating force that frees me from an addiction that — for the sex abuser — is more enslaving and loveless than drugs or alcohol. And even more, chastity will develop in me a love power that enables me to know and achieve the real purpose of marriage and find with my spouse the fullness of trust and confidence that are the foundation for a truly happy and lasting marriage.

Holy Orders, the Priesthood

65. What is the Sacrament of Holy Orders?

Holy Orders is the sacrament in which certain men are given the power and the graces of the priesthood. The word *orders* refers to the various levels of the priesthood, such as "the order" of episcopacy (bishops), "the order" of priesthood, "the order" of diaconate (deacons). The bishop has the fullness of the priesthood. Priests assist the bishop. Deacons assist both the bishop and the priests in their ministry. At first, it may seem that Holy Orders as a sacrament has nothing to do with the word *orders* as I know it in military service. But there is a great similarity. To be ordained to the priesthood is "to receive a set of orders" to serve the people in their spiritual needs, to defend them against the forces of evil, and to provide them with the opportunity for peace and justice. And since there is no love without justice, this opportunity to serve enables the people to fulfill the purpose of life, which is love!

Jesus himself issued "a set of orders" to his Apostles and to all priests when he said, "As the Father has sent me, so I send you" (John 20.21). Again it was a "set of orders" when Jesus said, "Full authority has been given to me both in heaven and on earth; go, therefore, and make disciples of all the nations. Baptize them in the name of the Father, and of the Son, and of the Holy Spirit. Teach them to carry out everything I have commanded you. And know that I am with you always, until the end of the world!" (Matthew 28.18-20).

Holy Orders is a sacrament because in becoming a priest a person takes on new responsibilities and needs the grace of this outward sign instituted by Jesus Christ for a greater share in his divine life. *(Hebrews 5.1-5)*

66. How does a priest become a military chaplain?

All military chaplains volunteer for the service. With the permission of his own bishop or religious superior, a priest applies to the military vicar, who is the Catholic bishop in charge of all Catholic chaplains and all Catholic personnel in the armed forces. With the approval of the military vicar, the priest then applies to the branch of the armed forces he wishes to enter. If accepted, he attends a chaplains' school and receives his first set of orders. Army and Air Force chaplains are usually commissioned as First Lieutenants; Navy chaplains are usually commissioned as Lieutenants Junior Grade. The United States Marines and the Coast Guard are served by Navy chaplains.

67. Do men in the military service ever end up becoming priests?

As a matter of fact, quite a few men have entered the seminary after finishing their time in the service and go on to become priests. Some of them are as young as twenty-two or as old as forty-two. Some are even younger and a few even older. The initial requirements are a high-school diploma, maturity, a balanced personality, a willingness to work and study, and the determination to develop a strong, Christian character. How long it takes depends on how much education a person already has. To be ordained to the priesthood, a man needs four years of college, which includes philosophy, and four years of theology. It may sound like a tough program, but it is worth every minute of it. As one ex-serviceman said when he was ordained, "I never thought I could make it, but I never thought I could be this happy either!"

If I am interested in becoming a priest, I should talk with the Catholic chaplain or write to the Military Archdiocese, 962 Wayne Avenue, Silver Spring, MD 20910.

68. Why can't women be ordained to the priesthood?

Frankly, the Church doesn't even know why certain men are ordained to the priesthood. Oh, the Church knows "for what purpose" men are ordained. But why *this* man or *that* man is chosen for the priesthood is just not known. What we do know is that no one is worthy to be a priest. No one has a *right* to receive the Sacrament of Holy Orders. Certainly, no one can "demand" to receive the priesthood. The priesthood is not received for oneself but for others. For the present, the Church is following the example of Jesus and the Apostles who apparently did not ordain any women to the priesthood. The vocation to the priesthood is one of the minor mysteries in the Catholic religion. Although books have been written on "Why I Became a Priest," the overall conclusion is that *no* priest really knows exactly why or how he was called by God to be a priest.

I do know there are two elements involved. The first is the natural ability to do the work of a priest plus the willingness on the part of the candidate (no one is ever forced to be a priest), and secondly, the acceptance by the bishop.

Women should not feel neglected or discriminated against in this matter any more than the men who do not receive a vocation from God or the approval of the bishop. *(Hebrews 5.4-5)*

Whenever a young woman thinks she may have an interest in or finds herself curious about life in the convent, she may choose first to talk it over with the Catholic chaplain, especially if there is no religious sister available. Or she may choose to visit a local convent. Most convents are pleased to welcome interested young women even if they are only curious. Some convents may extend an invitation to stay for a weekend to experience firsthand what the religious life is like. Most Catholic magazines and newspapers contain addresses to which a young woman may write for information about requirements and qualifications. When a young woman first gets the idea (even remotely) that she might consider entering the convent, she is likely to regard the idea as absolutely crazy! That's when she should remember that about seventy-five percent of the sisters in the convent probably felt the same way until they discovered the beauty and thrill of perfect love in consecrating their lives to God in the service of humankind.

The Anointing of the Sick

69. My uncle died a few months ago. My mother wrote and said he had received "the last sacraments." What are the last sacraments?

When a Catholic is critically or seriously ill, Jesus reaches out with an abundance of grace through three sacraments that help the person deal with his suffering and, if necessary, prepare him for a happy and peaceful death. The first is the Sacrament of Penance (Reconciliation) in which the priest helps the patient to make a good confession, clear up any doubts or worries the patient may have about his life, and receive forgiveness once again for all the sins of his past.

Secondly, the patient receives Holy Communion. This is also called *viaticum,* which may be translated loosely "I am on the way with you." The patient is reminded that he is united with Jesus in this sacrament and need not fear that he is alone in facing illness or death.

Thirdly, the patient receives the Sacrament of the Anointing of the Sick. In this sacrament, the priest anoints the patient with blest oil and prays for a restoration of health or, if that is not God's will, for the grace and courage to bear the illness in union with Jesus, whose death on the cross was more than anyone is asked to bear. Finally, the patient is given a special apostolic blessing, which is the blessing given in the name of the pope as if the pope himself were giving the blessing.

These "last sacraments" often improve the physical condition of the patient. This healing power is not always a miracle. The peace of mind and the relaxed confidence that the sacraments produce in the patient often enables nature to heal itself.

(James 5.14-15)

70. Do I have to be dying to receive the Sacrament of the Anointing of the Sick?

No, I do not have to be dying to receive the sacrament of the sick. I can receive this sacrament everytime I am seriously ill.

71. How many times can I receive the sacraments?

I can receive the Sacraments of Baptism, Confirmation, and Holy Orders only once.

The Sacrament of Matrimony can be received again after the death of one's spouse.

The Sacrament of the Anointing of the Sick can be received during each serious illness.

The Sacraments of Holy Communion and Penance may be received as often as I wish. Holy Communion is usually received only once a day. However, I can receive Holy Communion a second time as part of my participation in another Mass. Of course, if I have committed a serious sin, I may not receive Holy Communion until I have gone to Confession.

I must also be in the "state of grace," that is, without serious sin, when I receive the Sacrament of Confirmation, Matrimony, or Holy Orders.

Devotion to Mary and the Saints

72. Why was I taught to have devotion to Mary the mother of Jesus and to the other saints?

It's all in the Bible. In the Gospel of St. Luke, chapter 1, verses 28 through 50, Mary is called "blessed among women," and "favored" of God. The angel said to Mary, "You shall conceive and bear a son and give him the name Jesus . . . and the holy offspring to be born will be called Son of God." And in verse 48, "All ages to come shall call me blessed."

That is why I honor and love Mary, because (after Jesus) she is the holiest and most blessed human being who ever lived; because she is, as the Bible says, so favored by God; and because her son, Jesus, is the Son of God.

That rightfully gives her the title of Mother of God. (Of course, Mary did not "give birth to God" any more than my mother gave birth to my soul. But she is still *my* mother, not just the mother of my body. Mary is the mother of Jesus. And Jesus is personally God, the second person of the Blessed Trinity, who became man for our salvation. Therefore, Mary is properly honored and loved as the Mother of God.)

At the end of his life, Jesus gave us Mary as the mother of all Christians and all mankind when from the cross he said to St. John, "There is your mother." Jesus knew human nature well enough to know how much we needed a heavenly mother as well as a loving redeemer like himself.

Catholics do not worship Mary or the saints. We worship *only* God the Father, God the Son, and God the Holy Spirit. We *honor* and *respect* and pray with and through Mary and the saints because we are all part of the human family and are "all in this thing together." We know from the Bible that Mary and the early saints helped their friends when they were on earth. (Remember Mary at the wedding feast of Cana?) Now that they are in heaven, there is no reason to think that Mary and the saints are not just as loving and helpful as they were before, when they were on earth.

I have difficulty understanding people who say they love Jesus, but refuse to respect and honor his mother. When violent people hate someone, they are inclined to call that person names that are an insult to his mother. To offend a person's mother is regarded as the fiercest type of insult. I don't appreciate anyone who insults my friends, much less my mother. Jesus doesn't either.

---

73. What about the statues, medals, holy cards, and paintings used in Catholic churches and homes?

Catholics use these things the same way Americans use statues of heroes in Washington or in the town square. Pictures and medals are used for the same reason I have a picture of my mother, a ring from my girl friend, or an autograph of my favorite baseball player.

Mary and the saints are our heroes who have lived a life of love successfully and are now enjoying the glory of heaven. Those statues and pictures are *not* idols. They do *not* go against the First Commandment, which forbids false gods. They are simply reminders, like statues in a hall of fame, that someone like me followed Jesus successfully and that I can too.

Heaven
and
Hell

74. What or who are the angels?

The Bible mentions angels as
messengers of God and protectors of
men. *(Tobit 5; Luke 1.26; Revelations
10.1; 12.7).* I know from what is said in
the Bible that the angels are thinking,
loving persons like me, but they were
created outside the family of man. They
are called "pure spirits" to indicate that
they are not made up of body and soul as I
am. Not too much is really known about
the angels except that they *do* exist and
that they *are* interested in the welfare of
mankind.

*(Revelation 12.11-12; Psalms 103.20;
Matthew 18.10)*

75. Do I have to believe that the devil exists?

I better believe it. In the military, one of the greatest weapons is camouflage — the effort to make the enemy think I do not exist. The devil uses this for all it's worth in trying to make me think *he* does not exist. The Bible makes many references to "the forces of evil" or the "evil one." Jesus was tempted by the devil and a number of times drove "the devil" out of people. Jesus used the name *Satan* to refer to the "power of evil." In the Book of Revelation (12.7), St. John says the devil is a fallen angel. Yes, I better believe the devil exists and be prepared to deal with his clever temptations.

(Luke 10.18; Isaiah 14.12-15; Revelation 12.7-9)

76. Do I "have" to believe in heaven and hell?

Yes, unless I am prepared to say that there is no difference between loving and not loving. Heaven is a state of perfect love. Hell is a state of perfect lovelessness — absolutely *no* love! That may not sound very exciting or frightening at first. But just imagine what this world would be like if everyone *really* loved one another.

On the other hand, and with the condition of the world today, it might be easier to imagine what this world would be like if everyone — I mean everyone — hated one another.

Both ideas, of course, are impossible in the present world of time. But heaven and hell are not in time, they are in eternity. Just *where* heaven and hell are is beyond my imagination simply because we do not know many details about eternity. Besides, "knowing where" heaven and hell are would only satisfy my curiosity, not help me fulfill my purpose in life.

To think, as some atheists claim, that heaven and hell are merely inventions to encourage or frighten people into practicing religion is as stupid and absurd as saying that knowledge and ignorance are inventions to encourage or frighten people into education.

(1 Corinthins 2.1-16)

77. If God is so good and loving, why did he create hell, and how can he condemn anyone to hell?

God did not create hell any more than "Mr. Goodyear" or "Mr. Firestone" created the flat tire. The person who runs over a nail creates the flat tire. God created me for love and for heaven. The first person who refused to love created hell. That person, according to St. John (Revelation 12.7) was Lucifer, the archangel, now known as Satan, or the devil.

Furthermore, God does not condemn anyone to hell. Anyone who goes to hell condemns himself to hell by choosing not to love. That's why to sin is the failure to love, and to die "in the state of mortal sin" is to reject the God of love and refuse to love him or anyone else — forever. That's hell!

(Wisdom 1.13-15)

Prayer

78. What is the best way to pray?

The best way to pray depends on where
I am, what I am doing, and what's going
on inside me. The best definition of
prayer is still "the lifting of the mind and
heart to God." In fact, that also describes
a good conversation with a friend. In a
good conversation, I reveal my mind or
my heart or both to my friend. And
prayer is a conversation with God.

Sometimes I can use words that
someone else made up or prayers taken
from the Bible, such as the Our Father or
the Psalms. Some prayers are adapted
from the Bible, like the Hail Mary or the
Glory Be to the Father. These prayers

are particularly good when I am praying with others.

Prayers written by others should be a springboard to get me started praying in my own words. When I pray, I ought to talk with God the way I talk with someone I love, with my Dad or my Mother, or a good friend. No fancy words. No clever phrases. I just tell God how I feel, what I've been doing, and how things turned out. I can thank God for his blessings and tell him how great I think he is. Yes, I can even complain to God. I can gripe. I can ask for help. I can even argue with God, and when I am distracted in my prayer, I can tell him about the distractions.

But I must remember that prayer is a conversation. It's two-sided. So I need to be quiet once in a while and just listen. Listening in prayer may well be the more important part. I know God isn't going to talk to me in a rumble of thunder. That's why I need to get off by myself at times, turn off the blaring music, get away from it all and just . . . listen . . . and think . . . and listen.

Perhaps I can pick up the Gospels and let Jesus talk to me through his words

that I read there. I might hear even more
than is written there. Jesus wasn't
kidding when he said, "He who has ears
to hear me, let him hear!" Just as there
are many ways to have a conversation
with a friend, so there are a variety of
ways to pray. Sometimes I use words.
Sometimes I just relax in God's
presence. Sometimes I just listen. But
however I pray I know that prayer keeps
me alive and well . . . and aware that I
am never alone!
(Matthew 6.5-15; 11.28; 28.20)

---

79. What are some of the prayers frequently used by Catholics that I probably should know by heart.

The three most popular prayers that
Catholics usually know by heart are the
Our Father, the Hail Mary, and the Glory
Be to the Father.

The Lord's Prayer
Our Father, who art in heaven, hallow-
ed be thy name; thy kingdom come; thy
will be done on earth as it is in heaven.
Give us this day our daily bread; and for-

give us our trespasses as we forgive those who trespass against us; and lead us not into temptation, but deliver us from evil. Amen.

Hail Mary
Hail Mary, full of grace! The Lord is with you. Blessed are you among women, and blessed is the fruit of your womb, Jesus.

Holy Mary, Mother of God, pray for us sinners, now and at the hour of our death. Amen.

Glory Be to the Father
Glory to the Father, and to the Son, and to the Holy Spirit. As it was in the beginning, is now, and ever shall be, world without end. Amen.

There are other prayers that I as a Catholic ought to be familiar with and try to know by heart, especially those used in the Mass, like the Glory to God in the Highest and the Nicene Creed. These prayers and others, including the Apostles' Creed, prayers after Communion, and the prayers of the rosary, I can find at the end of this booklet. (See: "Prayers to Help Me Pray Better," p. 108.)

One more thing about prayer. I should never forget how important it is to pray for others. It's not that I am going to tell God something he doesn't already know about the needs of others, it's just that in asking and expressing my needs and the needs of others I am giving expression to my love for God and for my neighbor and declaring my faith and trust in God's goodness.

In praying for my relatives and friends who have died, I remind myself again that we are all one human family and that death does not end this relationship. Death only changes the manner in which some of us are living. I remember reading in the Old Testament (see 2 Maccabees 12.42-46) that people way back then prayed for the dead that they might be freed from their sins. That condition in which those who have died still need to be freed from some sin is what I as a Catholic call "purgatory." I know that some people say they do not believe in purgatory. Perhaps it is because they do not really understand what purgatory is all about. One thing is for sure, no one can deny that Judas Maccabeus "made atonement for the dead that they might be freed from this sin." And I know that I can do the same for my relatives and friends *(2 Maccabees 12.46)*

I also need to remind myself as a Catholic that my Church is a praying Church! That is what the words *liturgy* and *liturgical* mean. When we celebrate Mass, the sacraments, or the divine office (the official morning, noon, and evening prayers of the Church), we offer prayers of worship, praise, and thanks to our heavenly Father as well as ask for help and favors. This praying together is the liturgical life of the Church, and while the truths taught by Jesus will never change, I shouldn't be surprised when the prayerful response to those truths changes to meet my needs in today's world — like the change from Latin to English — to help me be more active in the liturgical life of my Church.

How the Church Works

80. What is the "chain of command" in the Catholic Church?

Any large group of people with a mission or a job to do requires organization. When the Church was small, the organization was simple. Today, there are over 795 million Catholics in the world. The larger the group, the more structured the organization needs to be. To make sure things happen the way they are supposed to happen, an organization needs leaders.

Jesus knew human nature well. He recognized the need for leadership when he appointed St. Peter to lead the

Apostles. The pope is the successor of St. Peter, the vicar, or chief representative, of Jesus Christ on earth. Just as St. Peter was the leader of the Apostles, so the pope is the leader of all the bishops, who are the successors of the Apostles.

When there is any question or doubt about what Catholics ought to believe or do to be truly Christian, the pope has the final word. The pope is the spiritual father of everyone in the whole world who is trying to be holy as Jesus taught us to be holy. That's why the pope is sometimes called "the Holy Father."

Next "in command" are the archbishops and bishops. An archbishop is the leader of a large area known as an archdiocese. A bishop is the leader of a smaller area known as a diocese.

Each archbishop or bishop is assisted by a group of priests. The priest is the leader of a parish, which is a group of people in a neighborhood. A parish can be fairly small or very large.

There are also bishops, called auxiliary bishops, who assist other bishops or do staff work in special fields. The pope has quite a few bishops on his staff in Rome.

The bishop of a very large diocese may have one or several auxiliary bishops.

A cardinal is a bishop or a priest who has been honored by the pope with that title either because of the importance of his diocese or because he has a special job. The cardinals also have the privilege of electing the pope.

A monsignor is a priest who has been given that title by the pope in recognition of his outstanding work or his important position.

Permanent deacons assist bishops and priests. A temporary deacon is a student for the priesthood in his final stage before ordination to the priesthood.

81. What are the laws of the Catholic Church? Are these the same as the "Commandments of the Church?"

The laws of the Catholic Church are contained in a rather large book known as the "Code of Canon Law." There are 1,752 rules and regulations governing just about every activity in the Church. This is a "handbook" that the leaders of the Church use to insure that everything is done properly and that everyone is treated justly.

The "Commandments of the Church" (sometimes called the Precepts of the Church) are certain special duties that I as a Catholic am required to do in order to fulfill God's more general Ten Commandments. They are the following:

1. To keep holy the day of the Lord's resurrection; to worship God by participating in Mass every Sunday and Holy Day of Obligation; to avoid activities that would hinder renewal of soul and body on the Sabbath (for example, needless work and business activities, unnecessary shopping, etc.)

The Holy Days of Obligation in the United States are:
- January 1 — Solemn Feast of Mary, Mother of God
- Feast of the Ascension (40 days after Easter)
- August 15 — The Assumption of Mary into Heaven
- November 1 — All Saints Day
- December 8 — Feast of the Immaculate Conception
- December 25 — Christmas Day

2. To lead a sacramental life; to receive Holy Communion frequently and the Sacrament of Penance regularly — at least to receive the Sacrament of Penance once a year (annual confession is an obligation if serious sin is involved); also to receive Holy Communion at least once a year between the first Sunday of Lent and Trinity Sunday. (This is known as the Easter duty.)

3. To study Catholic teaching in preparation for the Sacrament of Confirmation, to be confirmed, and then to continue to study and advance the cause of Christ.

4. To observe the marriage laws of the Church; to give religious training, by example and word, to one's children; to use parish schools and catechetical programs.

5. To strengthen and support the Church, that is, one's own parish community and parish priests, the worldwide Church, and the pope.

6. To do penance, including abstaining from meat and fasting from food on the appointed days.

On a day of fasting, only one full meal is permitted. The other two meals may not equal a full meal. At present, there are only two days of fasting: Ash Wednesday and Good Friday. Catholics between the ages of twenty-one and fifty-nine are obliged to fast. Abstaining from meat including meat products is required on Ash Wednesday and all the Fridays of Lent including Good Friday. This can be changed by the local bishop. All Catholics over the age of fourteen are obliged to abstain from meat on the designated days.

I can consult my Catholic chaplain about special circumstances that may lessen or eliminate my obligation in some of these matters.

7. To join in the missionary spirit and apostolate of the Church. This includes helping in the Catholic chapel program at my duty station, visiting and helping priests, especially the missionaries when I am in a foreign country. This also includes learning more about my faith and sharing it with other Catholics and anyone else who might be interested.

Various Religions and Churches

82. Why are there so many "religions" in the world if there is only one God?

Mankind has always had a "deep suspicion" if not a conviction that there is more to life than what he sees around him. When someone knows about the one, true God, he will usually try to love and worship him. However, if man does not know the one, true God, or for some reason refuses to believe in him, then he will invent for himself a god or several gods.

In the beginning, as centuries began to separate mankind from his original creation, some people lost sight of the truth about God and began inventing their own gods. With the invention of these false gods came the invention of false religions. These religions were hardly ever totally wrong. At least they satisfied mankind's suspicion that there was more to life than met the eye. The similarities in the different religions simply indicate the reality that mankind had a common origin.

I must remember that a person is always free to accept or deny the truth about God. That freedom also enables anyone who rejects the truth to invent his own god and his own religion. For this reason, new religions are being invented almost everyday.

(Joshua 24.13-24)

---

83. But why are there so many Christian churches and denominations?

Christians are also free to accept or reject the truth about God and about his Son, Jesus. Even though the Catholic Church continues to grow every year, I also know that a number of Catholics are denying the truth and leaving the Church every year. Fortunately, they do not all start a new church. But in just about every century since the second century, people have been leaving the Catholic Church to start their own church. Many have not survived. Some have. That's a matter of history. It is also the price of freedom.

(Hebrews 3.12-19; Matthew 24.4-5)

---

84. Just how should I deal with people of other Christian faiths?

With love! Remember, being wrong or incomplete does *not* make me bad unless it is my own fault and I don't care. Failing to love is the mistake Christians made some four centuries ago. They tried to correct one another and ended up being angry with one another. In the end, they had trouble sorting out what was essential to the Church that Jesus started and what was no more than custom, culture, or actually abuse. Once some of these people were cut off from the leadership of the pope, they began to use personal religious experience as the norm of truth, and that always leads to endless fragmentation, or breaking into small groups.

I am a Catholic because I know the

Catholic Church teaches the total message of Jesus and possesses the fullness of opportunity for salvation through the seven sacraments. But I must love and have a caring respect for those who, for whatever reason, are not so fortunate as to share in this fullness. What we need today is to love one another and be able to talk calmly with one another about what is truly the will of God. I must *never* "argue about religion" in anger. I need to study my Catholic faith as an adult and show my friends that what I believe is what Jesus taught and what his disciples recorded in the Bible.
(Romans 8.35-39)

---

85. A friend of mine made a strange statement the other day. He said, "I used to be a Catholic, now I am a Christian." Just what did he mean?

As the saying goes in the military, he may have been trying to "shake up the troops." Or he may merely have been trying to justify himself. Whatever his motives, the statement may be saying something I ought to hear!

As a Catholic, I may be trying to survive on what I learned as a kid, with a pretty slim knowledge of what it really means to be a Catholic. Or, I may know my Catholic religion very well, but I forget that I am supposed to *live* the truth, the love, and the justice that the Church teaches.

All the teaching in the Bible, all the sacraments, all the Catholic practices, all the Catholic customs, everything I am and do as a Catholic must be aimed at the fulfillment of the one "great" commandment of love!

Your friend may have been in a Catholic parish or with a group of Catholics who were cold, unfeeling, uncaring, and thoughtless of one another. The Mass and the sacraments and Catholic devotions may have been nothing more to them than empty gestures without any real meaning. Your friend may have found a group outside the Catholic Church who, even with an incomplete grasp of the Christian faith, were kind, thoughtful, caring, and concerned. They seemed to know and mean what they were doing. He may have thought to himself, *"This* is the way I think Christians ought to act." And he was so right! His mistake was in not seeing the difference between how some Catholics act and what the Catholic Church teaches how they *should* act.

Perhaps this little book will help me not only to know more about my Catholic religion and encourage me to go on learning more, but I hope it will also remind me that the fruit of being a better Catholic is to be a better person, a better Christian, a more loving, more thoughtful, more kind, more caring neighbor to all my friends and fellow servicemen.

As an adult Catholic I "owe" the world one, mature, authentic Christian, capable of fulfilling that one, great requirement for being a Christian in which Jesus summarized his whole teaching:

"This is how all will know you for my disciples: your love for one another." "Love one another as I have loved you." (*John 13.34-35; 15.12*)

Prayers
to Help Me
Pray Better

I. Some of the Prayers Used at Mass

Confiteor

I confess to almighty God,
and to you, my brothers and sisters,
that I have sinned through my own fault
in my thoughts and in my words,
in what I have done,
and in what I have failed to do;
and I ask blessed Mary, ever Virgin,
all the angels and saints,
and you, my brothers and sisters,
to pray for me to the Lord our God.

Gloria

Glory to God in the highest,
and peace to his people on earth.

Lord, God, heavenly King,
almighty God and Father,
we worship you, we give you thanks,
we praise you for your glory.
Lord Jesus Christ, only Son of the Father,
Lord God, Lamb of God,
you take away the sin of the world:
have mercy on us;
you are seated at the right hand of the
Father:
receive our prayer.
For you alone are the Holy One,
you alone are the Lord,
you alone are the Most High,
Jesus Christ
with the Holy Spirit,
in the glory of God the Father.
Amen.

Nicene Creed

We believe in one God,
the Father, the Almighty,
maker of heaven and earth,
of all that is seen and unseen.
We believe in one Lord, Jesus Christ,
the only Son of God,
eternally begotten of the Father,
God from God, Light from Light,
true God from true God,

begotten, not made, one in Being with
the Father.

Through him all things were made.

For us men and for our salvation he
came down from heaven:

by the power of the Holy Spirit

he was born of the Virgin Mary, and
became man.

For our sake he was crucified under
Pontius Pilate;

he suffered, died, and was buried.

On the third day he rose again

in fulfillment of the Scriptures;

he ascended into heaven

and is seated at the right hand of the
Father.

He will come again in glory to judge the
living and the dead,

and his kingdom will have no end.

We believe in the Holy Spirit, the Lord,
the giver of life,

who proceeds from the Father and the
Son.

With the Father and the Son he is
worshiped and glorified.

He has spoken through the Prophets.

We believe in one holy catholic and
apostolic Church.

We acknowledge one baptism for the

forgiveness of sins.
We look for the resurrection of the
    dead,
and the life of the world to come.
    Amen.

Prayer Over the Gifts

Priest: Pray, brethren, that our
sacrifice may be acceptable to God, the
almighty Father.

People: May the Lord accept the
sacrifice at your hands for the praise and
glory of his name, for our good, and the
good of all his Church.

At the Conclusion of the Preface

Holy, holy, holy Lord, God of power and
    might.
Heaven and earth are full of your glory.
Hosanna in the highest.
Blessed is he who comes in the name of
    the Lord.
Hosanna in the highest.

After the Our Father

For the kingdom, the power, and the
glory are yours, now and forever.

Breaking of the Bread

Lamb of God, you take away the sins of
    the world: have mercy on us.

Lamb of God, you take away the sins of
    the world: have mercy on us.

Lamb of God, you take away the sins of
    the world: grant us peace.

Before Communion

Priest: This is the Lamb of God who
takes away the sins of the world. Happy
are those who are called to his supper.
All: Lord, I am not worthy to receive
you, but only say the word and I shall be
healed.

II. Some Prayers to Know

Sign of the Cross

In the name of the Father, and of the
Son, and of the Holy Spirit. Amen.

Prayer for Today

My God, I offer you my prayers, works,
joys, and sufferings of this day in union
with the Sacred Heart of Jesus, for the
intentions for which he offers himself in
all the Holy Masses throughout the
world, in thanksgiving for favors and

blessings I have received in the past and in reparation for my sins and for the intentions of the Holy Father.

I renew my baptismal vows to be faithful to you, to renounce Satan and all his works, and to take Jesus Christ as my model and guide today and all the days of my life. Amen.

Act of Faith, Hope, and Love

My God, I believe that you are the one, true God in three divine persons; I believe in the birth, death, and resurrection of your divine Son, Jesus Christ; that he died for our sins and that he will judge us at the end of the world according to our works. I believe in the Holy Spirit, who continues to teach us the will of the Father and the words of Jesus through the Holy Catholic Church.

Heavenly Father, trusting in your goodness and mercy, I hope for the forgiveness of my sins, the continuing help of your grace, and eternal life with you and all those I have loved.

God the Father, God the Son, and God the Holy Spirit, always the One and Loving God, I love you above all things and love my neighbor as myself. I shall always try to be worthy of your love for me and to forgive all who may have offended me. I resolve to see you in all men and to treat every person with dignity, respect, and sincere love. Amen.

Prayer of Saint Francis

Lord, make me an instrument of your peace.

Where there is hatred, let me sow love;
Where there is injury, pardon;
Where there is doubt, faith;
Where there is despair, hope;
And where there is sadness, joy.

O Divine Master, grant that I may not so much seek to be consoled as to console; to be understood as to understand; to be loved as to love;

For it is in giving that we receive; it is in pardoning that we are pardoned; and it is in dying that we are born to eternal life.

Amen.

Prayer for Happiness in Marriage

Heavenly Father, you well know the sacrifices, problems, and hopes which come to all who embrace married life.

Give us all the graces we need to love

each other and unite our hearts in unselfish harmony so that mindful of the needs and wishes of each other, we can live our lives united to each other and to you as we share our lives with each other totally and exclusively.

Grant us the patience to deal with our problems and our faults so that we may constantly grow in our love for each other and for you. May we never violate our pledge of love and fidelity. And may we do your will in all things so that we may one day enjoy together the happiness of heaven with you. Amen.

Prayer to the Holy Spirit
O Holy Spirit, You are the bond of love between the Father and the Son. Be also the bond of love between me and those with whom I live and work and share my life, my talent, and my time. May I always listen to your voice and, through your guidance, be faithful in thought, word, and deed to all that is right and just. Amen.

Prayer to Mary,
Our Blessed Mother

Remember, O most gracious Virgin
Mary, that never was it known that
anyone who fled to your protection,
implored your help, or sought your
intercession, was left unaided. Inspired
with this confidence, I come to you, O
Virgin of virgins, my Mother; before you
I stand sinful and sorrowful. O Mother of
the Word Incarnate! Despise not my
petitions, but in your mercy hear and
answer me. Amen.

The Rosary of the Blessed Virgin Mary

The Rosary is a prayer of meditation
on some of the major events of the
history of salvation in the lives of our
Lord, Jesus Christ, and his Blessed
Mother, Mary. The Rosary is based on
the principle that when I think of
something for fifteen minutes a day it is
bound to influence my life. Thinking of
the life of Jesus and Mary for fifteen
minutes a day is almost certain to
influence my life for the better,
strengthen my faith, help me grow in
love power, and become a more mature,
thinking, loving person.

For the Rosary to have this effect in my life, I must remember that the important part of this prayer is the meditation on the various scenes, or "mysteries," of the Rosary. Perhaps these scenes are called "mysteries" because they reflect the great mystery of God's love for me. Anyway, there are fifteen of these mysteries, and I need to learn what each one means so that I can use a simple method of meditation with each one — the "see, catch, apply" method. I "see" the picture or the scene; I "catch" the lesson in the scene; and I "apply" the lesson to my own life.

While meditating on each mystery or scene, I recite one Our Father and ten Hail Marys. These are like background music to help me absorb myself in the spirit of prayer, but they should never take the place of the meditation on the mysteries of the Rosary.

Ordinarily when I pray the Rosary, I meditate on only five of the fifteen mysteries. That's why the fifteen mysteries are divided into three groups known as the "Joyful Mysteries," the "Sorrowful Mysteries," and the "Glorious Mysteries."

The Joyful Mysteries
1. *The Annunciation:* The Angel
   Gabriel announces to Mary that she is
   to be the Mother of the Messiah
   (Jesus). Mary freely accepts and
   submits to God's will.
2. *The Visitation:* Bearing the child
   Jesus in her womb, Mary visits her
   cousin Elizabeth who is waiting to give
   birth to her son, John the Baptizer. On
   this occasion Mary is first called
   "Blest among women" (Luke 1.42).
3. *The Birth of Our Lord, Jesus:* The
   child Jesus is born poor and
   unrecognized in a stable-cave in
   Bethlehem.
4. *The Presentation:* In accord with
   Jewish law and custom, Mary and
   Joseph present Jesus in the Temple
   and offer him to God.
5. *The Finding of Jesus in the
   Temple:* When Jesus was twelve
   years old, his parents took him to visit
   the Temple. They got separated in the
   crowd. When Mary and Joseph found
   Jesus, he was teaching in the Temple.
   "All who heard him were amazed at
   his intelligence and his answers"
   (Luke 2.47).

The Sorrowful Mysteries

1. *The Agony in the Garden:* Jesus accepts the suffering and his coming death on the cross for our redemption. After sweating blood he said: "Let it be as you would have it, not as I."

2. *The Scourging:* The soldiers flog Jesus unmercifully. The Roman scourging was done with a whip much like the "cat-o'-nine-tails."

3. *Jesus Is Crowned With Thorns:* A crown of thorns is painfully placed on Jesus' head in mockery of him who called himself "King of the Jews."

4. *Jesus Carries the Cross:* In his weakened condition, Jesus is forced to carry his cross to the top of Calvary. He was helped by a stranger, Simon of Cyrene.

5. *Jesus Dies on the Cross:* With only his mother and the Apostle John to share his suffering, Jesus offers the hours on the cross to his Father in reparation for our sins. Finally he commended his soul to the Father and died.

The Glorious Mysteries

1. *The Resurrection:* Jesus having

conquered sin and death once for all,
rose from the dead to a new, glorious,
and eternal life.

2. *The Ascension:* After spending
   some time with his disciples as the
   Risen Lord, Jesus returns to the
   Father in heaven.

3. *The Descent of the Holy Spirit:* As
   he promised, Jesus sends his Spirit to
   his disciples, and the Church begins its
   mission of bringing the good news of
   salvation to all men of all nations.

4. *The Assumption of Mary:* When
   her time on this earth was completed,
   Mary was taken bodily into heaven by
   her son.

5. *The Crowning of the Blessed
   Virgin:* Because she gave life to
   Jesus, the Savior of the world and the
   life of all the redeemed, Our Lady is
   acknowledged as Queen of all in
   heaven and on earth.

Apostles' Creed

I believe in God, the Father almighty,
Creator of heaven and earth; and in Jesus
Christ, his only Son, our Lord, who was
conceived by the Holy Spirit, born of the
Virgin Mary, suffered under Pontius

Pilate, was crucified, died, and was buried. He descended into hell; the third day he arose again from the dead. He ascended into heaven and sits at the right hand of God, the Father almighty; from thence he shall come to judge the living and the dead.
I believe in the Holy Spirit, the holy Catholic Church, the communion of saints, the forgiveness of sins, the resurrection of the body, and life everlasting. Amen.

Prayers After Holy Communion

Behold O kind and most sweet Jesus, I cast myself upon my knees in your sight, and with the most fervent desire of my soul, I pray and beseech you that you would impress upon my heart lively sentiments of faith, hope, and charity, with true repentance for my sins, and a firm desire of amendment, while with deep affection and grief of soul I ponder within myself and mentally contemplate your five most precious wounds, having before my eyes that which David spoke in prophecy of you, O good Jesus; "They have pierced my hands and my feet; they have numbered all my bones."

Soul of Christ, sanctify me.
Body of Christ, save me.
Blood of Christ, inebriate me.
Water from the side of Christ, wash me.
Passion of Christ, strengthen me.

O good Jesus, hear me.
Within your wounds hide me.
Suffer me not to be separated from you.
From the malignant enemy, defend me.
In the hour of my death, call me and
bid me to come to you, that with your
saints, I may praise you forever and
ever. Amen.

O Lord, may your Body and Blood that I
have received in Holy Communion
adhere to the very depths of my soul.
May no trace of sin remain in me, whom
these pure and holy mysteries have
renewed.
O God, who live and reign for ever and
ever, be with me always and everywhere.
Amen.